RESILIENCY GUIDES

LIVING
THROUGH LOSS

A Guided Journal for the Pathway Forward

Janine Wilburn

WEST
MARGIN
PRESS

This is my story.
It is uniquely mine now and forever.
My triumphs and challenges,
my hopes and dreams,
my loves and heartbreaks,
my commitments and responsibilities.
My laughter and joy
captured here to be reflected on
now and in the future with
much compassion and gratitude.

—J. Wilburn

This journal belongs to

_____

Compassion is the heart's response to sorrow. We share in the beauty of life and in the ocean of tears. The sorrow of life is part of each of our hearts and part of what connects us with one another. It brings with it tenderness, mercy, and an all-embracing kindness that can touch every being.

—Jack Kornfield

CONTENTS

In life, loss is inevitable. Everyone knows this, yet at the core of most people it remains deeply denied— "This should not happen to me." It is for this reason that loss is the most difficult challenge one has to face as a human being.

—Dayananda Saraswati

INTRODUCTION

Welcome to Living Through Loss

This guided resilience journal is carefully crafted to provide you with daily support as you navigate through your loss. It may be the devastating loss of a loved one through death, or a breakup of a marriage or relationship. It could be the loss of your health and well-being, a job, your home or financial means, or the loss of a friendship, a trusted advisor's counsel, or a community. It could be the inability to spend time in person with your family and friends. It can be the loss associated with the closure of schools, workplaces, restaurants, coffee shops, or favorite venues. Living with loss can seem like an overwhelming, daunting, and insurmountable challenge. So how can you manage the emotional upset, mental turmoil, and the physical pain? How can you journey forward?

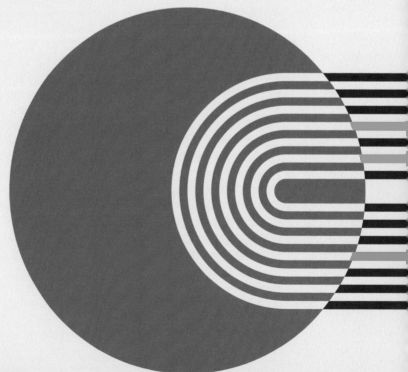

Coping with Loss

This book walks you through a number of practices and techniques to support you on your pathway to healing and recovery. There are some simple practices that you can incorporate into your daily life that will help ease the pain. Research in the area of neuroplasticity reveals how different thought patterns affect the human mind and body. Certain thoughts and actions naturally trigger the brain to release endorphins and hormones that positively impact the health and well-being of both the mind and the body. Based on science and my personal experience, this book is designed to engage you in easy, enjoyable, inspiring, and creative resilience-building activities to help you deal with your loss and grief.

Why I Created This Journal

Resiliency plays a critical role in my daily life and in my family's life. Twenty-four years ago, I was in a serious car accident. I experienced severe spinal injuries and was given a grim prognosis. This was when I first encountered the distinction in neuroscience called neuroplasticity, through Sharon Begley's book *Train Your Mind, Change Your Brain* and her exploration of Dr. Richard Davidson's research at the University of Wisconsin-Madison (my alma mater). I read and reread the book, and then studied everything I could find on the subject. I knew there were answers in the science to help me heal when most of my doctors and health care practitioners no longer believed it was possible.

I began to engage and develop daily practices that eventually were identified through research as the building blocks of resiliency. The results were overwhelmingly positive. My pain started to diminish, and sleep was available for a few hours at a time. I discovered that by being creative I could significantly minimize my pain, so I became a visual artist, even though I had limited use of my hands and arms at the time.

I dug deeper into observing, monitoring, and utilizing my thoughts to enhance my healing, and combined that knowledge and intention to create my many daily practices. In pursuit of a "cure," I found so much more. I learned the importance of love when dealing with hardship. I learned love comes in so many shapes and sizes: forgiveness, gratitude, kindness, creativity, acts of service, authentic listening, compassion, daily practices, prayer, meditation, yoga, still and quiet moments, exercise, and healthy eating.

My favorite go-to tool is gratitude, because I can use it anywhere and at any time. It has gotten me through incredibly challenging times. If my gratitude journal is not nearby, I will say gratitude statements out loud or in my mind, helping me to deal with everything from physical pain, and emotional upset to mental fatigue and overwhelm, whether that comes from aspects of my life or our collective lives. Writing this journal during a global pandemic, record breaking wildfires, political unrest, and needed social change heightened my awareness of just how much we all need gratitude in our lives and our world.

Although my sought-after "return to normal" has not materialized, I am deeply grateful.

I have learned so much, gained so much knowledge and maybe a little wisdom. I learned a new definition of hope—our only opportunity for control. That real, open-hearted connection is critical; that gratitude is one of our greatest tools; and that being of service is one of our greatest gifts. I learned to never stop trying and to never give up. I learned to appreciate every day and work to be present and conscious in the moment.

I have so much—my family who inspires me every day, my dedicated teachers who continue to support me, the people who allow me to be of service in their lives, my daily practices, and the many, many aspects of love. All these help me to continuously create and shape a life I love and am passionate about. I learned we never really know what the next moment or twenty-four years have in store for us; however, with our minds and our practices, we can make it something special.

How to Use This Book

One day at a time...

All you have is today, so be in the here and now. Lay down your pain and be in this moment on this day. As you contemplate what's next and how you are ever going to accomplish it, consider that you do not have to climb the mountain today. You can take it one step at a time, one hour at a time, and one day at a time.

Start at the beginning of the book and move your way through one or two pages a day. Pick a time of day that you are most likely to complete the page's activity. It could be first thing in the morning to get you going, or midday to provide a break from your daily routine. You could also choose to do your page in the evening before going to sleep. The most important aspect is to do at least one page per day. The daily interaction with the activities in the book can help mitigate and even diminish some sadness. The tools you'll learn can make the bright times brighter and the dark times lighter.

Tips

Here are some things to keep in mind as you move through this time of loss.

- GIVE YOURSELF SPACE to discover, understand, and adjust to the new normal.

- BE PATIENT WITH YOURSELF as you need time to recover from the loss. While tough times might feel like resistance to pressure or stress, it is usually that you need more recovery time in between.

- KEEP IT SIMPLE. Focus on one thing at a time. This is not a good time to multitask.

- QUIET TIME IS REQUIRED. Make sure to protect a certain amount of uninterrupted alone time every day. While your friends and family might miss you, explain to them that they will get a better You if you take some time alone.

- EXERCISE, EXERCISE, EXERCISE. It is not about how much you do, it is about doing something every day— whatever you can. Keep moving.

- TAKE TIME OFF SCREEN. Monitor how much time you are spending on your devices. Too much time can backfire and create more stress and upset.

- LIMIT YOUR CHOICES. Rebuild your tolerance for making and juggling choices, just like you would rebuild your muscles—a little at a time, and keep building.

- LEARN TO ASK FOR HELP, then gratefully accept the assistance. While you may be used to being more independent, now is the time to reach out more and accept more assistance. It takes strength to master this skill.

Courage doesn't always roar. Sometimes courage is the quiet voice at the end of the day saying, "I will try again tomorrow."
—Mary Anne Radmacher

FOR THE HARD DAYS

Everyone who has experienced loss knows the Hard Days. Those days when the grief, the missing, the feelings of aloneness just get to be too much—too heavy—all consuming. The resiliency tools and practices in this journal are designed to assist on these difficult days. However, there can be days when generating the energy to fill out even one page is too much, and for those days there is this section. So, let's begin with those times when you feel you can't generate the energy to fill out a page. Honestly, there will be days like that for most people.

Start at the beginning of the section and go from there. Sometimes it will take just a few pages to feel a positive shift. Other times you may find yourself going through the section multiple times. There is no right or wrong way to do this work; the helpful part is to engage with it.

THINGS TO HELP MYSELF FEEL BETTER

When our "new normal" includes dealing with loss, there are days when it is hard to get out of bed and do anything. You know, those days that really take it out of you. The activities on these pages can assist you during those difficult times, even during those dark moments.

Begin with the activity that calls to you or, in some cases, the activity that you find least offensive. If nothing is really speaking to you, start at the top of the list and work your way through the activities.

1. GRATITUDE. Make a list of five things you really like. It could be family members, friends, food, music, activities, and more. Quickly, list them down on paper or in your phone so you can easily look at it.

2. IMAGINE. Sing, dance, play, and be silly. Allow that childlike enthusiasm to surface and guide you into doing something just to do it. Something that you enjoy and makes you laugh. It does not have to be clever or sophisticated, it just has to be fun for you in the moment.

3. APPRECIATE. Smile at least five times today. If there are other people around, smile at them. Observe the power of the smile, both for you and for the recipient of the smile.

THINGS TO HELP MYSELF FEEL BETTER

4. CONNECT. Spend time with someone you care about. This can be in person, over the phone, or virtually. Reach out and connect today.

5. EAT HEALTHY. It may sound simple, but it works. Give your body the nutrients it needs, and it will respond gratefully.

6. EXERCISE. (You knew this one was coming!) Even on the hard days, it is really important to move. If it is for just five minutes, that's great—as long as the body is active in some way. If you set aside a certain time every day for movement, it will make doing the exercise easier.

7. EXPLORE. Be open to new things. Investigate something you have always wanted to learn about or something you have wanted to do but haven't done yet.

8. SERVICE. Help someone else today. It is remarkable how being of service can help you feel better in the moment.

GRATITUDE STATEMENTS

Read the gratitude statements on these pages out loud or in your head. Sometimes you might read a few quickly, and other times you might repeat all of them multiple times. It is absolutely okay if you don't feel grateful. Reading the statements is still helpful. In fact, people often report how difficult it is to get started. They are sure they can only do one statement, then find themselves doing more. Honor yourself and wherever you are today! Use the blank lines on the next page to add any of your own gratitude statements to the list.

I am grateful for feeling better.

I am grateful for having people who care about me.

I am grateful for any and all support I am receiving.

I am grateful for comforting hugs.

I am grateful for family.

I am grateful for all acts of kindness.

I am grateful to be able to help others.

I am grateful for my determination.

I am grateful for my sense of humor.

I am grateful for seeing the good in others.

I am grateful for good jokes.

I am grateful for keeping my cool today.

I am grateful for the vitality I have.

I am grateful for a hearty laugh.

GRATITUDE STATEMENTS

I am grateful for every day.

I am grateful for all the beauty in the world.

I am grateful for the sunrise.

I am grateful for fresh air.

I am grateful for a gorgeous sky.

I am grateful for a warm breeze.

I am grateful for a sunny day.

I am grateful for time outdoors.

I am grateful for the mountains.

I am grateful for the oceans.

I am grateful for the magnificent trees.

I am grateful for the sunset.

I am grateful for peaceful moments.

I am grateful for genuine caring.

_____

_____

_____

_____

_____

_____

_____

_____

GRATITUDE STATEMENTS

I am grateful for today.

I am grateful for my life.

I am grateful for my healing.

I am grateful for my resilience.

I am grateful for my talents.

I am grateful for being able to be me.

I am grateful for feeling better now.

I am grateful for being able to work now.

I am grateful for having faith in myself.

I am grateful for having the strength to never give up.

I am grateful for my courage to reach for the stars.

I am grateful for my hopes and dreams.

I am grateful for those who support me.

I am grateful for the smiles I receive.

GRATITUDE STATEMENTS

I am grateful for forgiving and being forgiven.

I am grateful for pursuing my dreams.

I am grateful for learning new lessons.

I am grateful for seeing the positive.

I am grateful for abundance.

I am grateful for new experiences.

I am grateful for a gentle hug.

I am grateful for others understanding
without needing explanation.

I am grateful for today's opportunities.

I am grateful for dreams of fancy.

I am grateful for creativity and imagination.

I am grateful for peaceful moments.

I am grateful for being me.

PERSONAL STATEMENTS

These statements work just like the gratitude statements but are even more personal. They reflect positive feelings one has or would like to have about oneself. Research reveals our thoughts affect our well-being, so read the statements below. Repeating them over and over can help build new plasticity and resilience.

I am loved.

I love myself as I am now.

I accept myself.

I forgive myself.

I release my fears.

I laugh every day.

I am free to enjoy.

I am heard and respected.

I am open to new experiences.

I give to and receive from my community.

I am at peace.

PERSONAL STATEMENTS

My past is complete.

My thoughts shape my experiences.

I notice the many rainbows on my path.

I listen with an open heart.

I find the calm in the storm.

I build strength every day.

I imagine inspiring possibilities.

I easily share with others.

I discover peace in the moment.

My day ends in gratitude.

We are all connected.

SMILE... CHUCKLE... LAUGH... LAUGH HARD

It is amazing how healing a smile, a chuckle, and a deep belly laugh can be in the moment and over time. When we learn to laugh as a favorite tool, it opens doors to joy when the doors were previously closed by pain or fear. So sometimes we just have to focus on smiling and laughing, even if we have to force it for a while.

Read the prompts here and write what comes to mind. Then return to these pages when you need a smile or pick-me-up.

I FOUND MYSELF SMILING WHEN:

_____

_____

_____

_____

_____

I CHUCKLED OVER:

_____

_____

_____

_____

_____

SMILE... CHUCKLE... LAUGH... LAUGH HARD

I REMEMBER LAUGHING ABOUT:

_____

_____

_____

_____

_____

I LAUGHED SO HARD, I COULDN'T STOP LAUGHING WHEN:

_____

_____

_____

_____

_____

There are only two days in the year that nothing can be done. One is called yesterday and the other is called tomorrow, so today is the right day to love, believe, do and mostly live.

—Dalai Lama [Tenzin Gyatso]

THE BRIDGE BACK— FINDING MY LIGHT

When you experience loss, it can feel like the light goes out and everything around you changes. Your foundation feels shaky, cracked, even destroyed. How are you going to keep going? This section gently guides you through activities that will assist you in reconnecting with yourself, your loved ones, and your life.

FINDING MYSELF NOW

Identify the positive qualities that you see in yourself and that you'd like to see in yourself. Circle the words that describe you. Feel free to add words.

Generous   OPTIMIST   **Kind**

Ecstatic   **AMAZING**

ENTHUSIASTIC   GENTLE   VITAL

Silly   **Brave**   HIGH INTEGRITY

Athletic   Compassionate   **Strong**

Healthy   Endearing   Funny

Lucky   SENSITIVE   TRUTHFUL

Insightful   WISE   Radiant

IMAGINATIVE   PEACEFUL   ENERGETIC

THOUGHTFUL   *Abundant*   Special

Creative   One of a kind   **Joyful**

Honest   Innovative   Happy

Humorous   *Charming*   PROSPEROUS

HONORABLE   INSPIRING   Problem Solver

Gregarious   HARD WORKER

Dedicated   ENGAGING   Risktaker

COMMITTED   Appreciative

THOUGHTS THAT DESCRIBE ME

Discoveries in neuroscience continue to reveal the importance of our thoughts, like how they trigger physical responses in our bodies and impact overall health. Fill in the blanks here using the words you selected on the previous pages to describe yourself and how you see yourself growing. For example: *I am healthy, strong, and vital.* Then read and reread these sentences daily to help create overall positive well-being.

I am _____

I am _____

I am _____

I am _____

I am _____

I am _____

I am _____

THOUGHTS THAT DESCRIBE
HOW I FEEL NOW

My life is _____

As I grow, my life will be _____

_____

My work is _____

As I grow, my work will be _____

_____

My family is _____

As I grow, my family will be _____

_____

My relationships are _____

As I grow, my relationships will be _____

_____

My friends are _____

As I grow, my friends will be _____

_____

My community is _____

As I grow, my community will be _____

_____

THE SUPPORT & HELP THAT I HAVE

Asking for and receiving assistance during challenging times is simultaneously critical and difficult because when experiencing loss, feelings of vulnerability, isolation, and fear can also occur. All that can make it complicated to ask for help. On this page, list out the sources of support you have and the support you still need.

THIS IS THE SUPPORT AND HELP THAT I HAVE:

-
-
-
-
-
-
-
-
-
-

THE SUPPORT & HELP THAT I NEED

Think about how you are feeling right now. What would it look like if you could receive all the help you need? This page is for you only, so capture everything you are feeling. Write from your heart without constriction.

-
-
-
-
-
-
-
-
-

FORGIVENESS

Forgiveness is a powerful tool, particularly when one is dealing with the formidable emotions surrounding loss. It is common to experience regrets, the "woulda, coulda, shoulda" thoughts that come when journeying through the pain and grief. This is where forgiveness becomes critical. Forgiving oneself and others during this time can help provide peace and even serenity in place of the hurt and anxiety. Fill in this page with your deep hurts concerning losses in your life.

I forgive myself for _____

I forgive myself for _____

I forgive myself for _____

I forgive myself for _____

I forgive myself for _____

I forgive myself for _____

I forgive myself for _____

I forgive myself for _____

I forgive myself for _____

I forgive myself for _____

FORGIVENESS

Here, include transgressions you would like others to forgive you for having done.

_____ forgives me for _____

_____ forgives me for _____

_____ forgives me for _____

_____ forgives me for _____

_____ forgives me for _____

_____ forgives me for _____

_____ forgives me for _____

_____ forgives me for _____

_____ forgives me for _____

_____ forgives me for _____

FORGIVENESS

Here is your opportunity to release anger, upset, hurt, and pain around things that have happened to you. When we forgive, we let go and remove the shackles of others' bad behavior toward us and our loved ones. Forgiveness allows the pain to disintegrate and replaces it with freedom and joy.

I forgive _____ for _____

I forgive _____ for _____

I forgive _____ for _____

I forgive _____ for _____

I forgive _____ for _____

I forgive _____ for _____

I forgive _____ for _____

I forgive _____ for _____

I forgive _____ for _____

I forgive _____ for _____

FORGIVENESS

I forgive _____ for _____

I forgive _____ for _____

I forgive _____ for _____

I forgive _____ for _____

I forgive _____ for _____

I forgive _____ for _____

I forgive _____ for _____

I forgive _____ for _____

I forgive _____ for _____

I forgive _____ for _____

Cherish everything in your day that contributes to happiness: spending a special moment with a child, drinking a cup of your favorite coffee, joking with a co-worker, saving a rosebush from destruction. Happiness hides in life's small details. If you're not looking, it becomes invisible.

—Joyce Brothers

THE WORLD OF GRATITUDE

The power of gratitude is almost incomprehensible as it seems to be such a simple act of acknowledgment. In fact, gratitude has the ability to melt away difficulties by positively shifting our perspective, enhancing our well-being, and building resiliency. Gratitude is a way of living that provides comfort, direction, and perspective even in the face of great challenges. It is a powerful tool that allows one to stand in the face of loss, and even death, with strength and resilience.

The Science of Gratitude—or How Gratitude Works

As popular as gratitude is, it is often misunderstood. Many believe it is just a feeling that comes when someone is kind to you or something nice happens to you. Some equate it to finding the silver linings in life. These are aspects and qualities of gratitude, but they do not speak to the entirety of gratitude. Rather, gratitude is a highly efficient tool that supports our mental, emotional, physical, and spiritual bodies.

Neuroscientific research reveals that gratitude can be used to help with mood swings, anxiety, post-traumatic stress, and sleep challenges. That is why it is critical to understand that gratitude is not just an emotion—it is a tool that brings peace, even happiness, to pain and loss. Gratitude can help us dissolve challenges by positively shifting our perspective and our sense of well-being.

However, gratitude is not always easy. When facing overwhelming difficulties, pain, and deep loss, reaching for gratitude can feel more challenging than climbing Mount Everest. Whether the difficulties are aspects of one's personal life or our collective lives, gratitude helps relieve the stress.

According to Dr. Robert Emmons at the University of California at Davis, gratitude is a choice: "It means that we sharpen our ability to recognize and acknowledge the giftedness of life. It means that we make a conscious decision to see blessings instead of curses. It means that our internal reactions are not determined by external forces. That gratitude is a conscious decision does not imply that it is an easy decision... while gratitude is pleasant, it is not easy."

Since gratitude is a state of being, generating and repeating gratitude statements is helpful when you're upset, angry, or hurt, as well as when you are happy. You can express gratitude over things that have happened. For example: *I am grateful for having my favorite sandwich for lunch*. You can also express gratitude over things you would like to happen; these are called gratitude intentions. For example: *I am grateful for my new job that provides for all my needs and more.*

RETRAIN YOUR BRAIN WITH GRATITUDE

Gratitude is most powerful when it becomes part of your daily routine. Creating a gratitude practice by journaling daily gratitudes or writing daily gratitude lists helps build resiliency. So, pick a time of day to do your gratitude statements and stick to it. Some people find starting their days with their gratitude practice sets a strongly positive tone for the day. Others prefer to write their gratitude statements during the day. Many choose to write their gratitude statements in the evening before going to sleep for a better night's rest.

Below, fill in the blanks with five things that you can express gratitude for today.

I am grateful for _____

_____

I am grateful for _____

_____

I am grateful for _____

_____

I am grateful for _____

_____

I am grateful for _____

_____

RETRAIN YOUR BRAIN WITH GRATITUDE

Don't be surprised when there are times you don't want to write anything or that you are even irritated by the thought. On those days, commit to writing at least five statements. You can be grateful for anything. Remember, you don't have to feel grateful when you write your gratitude statements. People regularly self-report that they end up doing many more than five statements on those days and feeling better mentally, emotionally, and even physically.

On those really hard days when you feel you can't write any gratitudes, pick up your gratitude journal or lists, and read and reread your gratitudes from previous days.

Below, fill in the blanks with five things you desire from the past, today, or in the future. If you can think of only a few things, go ahead and repeat the same gratitudes.

I am grateful for _____

I am grateful for _____

I am grateful for _____

I am grateful for _____

I am grateful for _____

THE VALUE OF DAILY GRATITUDES

As the days pass, notice your gratitude practice moving from something new to something routine. Eventually, the routine will become a habit and it will be harder not to do your gratitude practice than to do it. Finally, the habit becomes a daily ritual—and that gratitude practice will last you a lifetime. It will be helpful when you're upset, angry, or hurt, as well as when you are happy.

When you are developing your gratitude practice, express gratitude over things that have happened and create gratitude intentions for things you would like to happen. There is no right or wrong way to be grateful or to do gratitude. The value is in doing it!

Fill these pages with people, places, or things from your life that you are grateful for. Do as many gratitude statements as you can when you sit down to write. If you fill out all the pages in one sitting, that is okay; if you write only a couple gratitudes a day, that is okay too. Remember, this is not about feeling grateful, it is about expressing appreciation for things in your life.

THE VALUE OF DAILY GRATITUDES

I am grateful for _____

I am grateful for _____

I am grateful for _____

I am grateful for _____

I am grateful for _____

I am grateful for _____

I am grateful for _____

I am grateful for _____

I am grateful for _____

I am grateful for _____

I am grateful for _____

I am grateful for _____

I am grateful for _____

I am grateful for _____

I am grateful for _____

THE GENEROSITY OF GRATITUDE

Write about people, things, events, and activities from your past that you are grateful for having experienced.

I am grateful for _____

I am grateful for _____

I am grateful for _____

I am grateful for _____

I am grateful for _____

I am grateful for _____

I am grateful for _____

I am grateful for _____

I am grateful for _____

I am grateful for _____

THE GENEROSITY OF GRATITUDE

Think about who and what has supported you during this journey. Name the people, organizations, and others who have assisted you as you heal.

I am grateful for _____ helping me by providing _____

I am grateful for _____ helping me by providing _____

I am grateful for _____ helping me by providing _____

I am grateful for _____ helping me by providing _____

I am grateful for _____ helping me by providing _____

I am grateful for _____ helping me by providing _____

I am grateful for _____ helping me by providing _____

I am grateful for _____ helping me by providing _____

I am grateful for _____ helping me by providing _____

I am grateful for _____ helping me by providing _____

MY GRATITUDE INTENTIONS

The gratitude statements you write in this section are different from the ones you just completed. Here, you will generate gratitude statements for what you desire in your life as if it currently exists. For example, if you are looking for a new place to live, you would write: *I am grateful for finding, securing and moving into my new home now*. Reread your gratitude intentions regularly to keep them in mind, and keep adding to them over time.

I am grateful for _____

I am grateful for _____

I am grateful for _____

I am grateful for _____

I am grateful for _____

I am grateful for _____

I am grateful for _____

I am grateful for _____

I am grateful for _____

I am grateful for _____

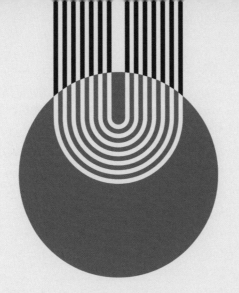

I am grateful for _____

I am grateful for _____

I am grateful for _____

I am grateful for _____

I am grateful for _____

I am grateful for _____

I am grateful for _____

I am grateful for _____

I am grateful for _____

I am grateful for _____

MY SEVEN-DAY GRATITUDE PRACTICE

Developing a daily practice is a gift. Begin by making a commitment to do resilience-building gratitude statements every day for one week. Notice as the practice moves from something that takes commitment, concentration, and work to something that is harder not to do than to do. Eventually, it will become a part of your daily life.

Fill in the blanks on these pages with people, things, and events you are grateful for today. On some days you might feel like adding more—do so. On the days when it is more difficult to fill in the blanks, remember that you can be grateful for everybody and everything. For example: *I am grateful for pizza!* You can also write gratitude intentions about what you'd like to create in your life. For example: *I am grateful for my raise now.*

DAY 1

I am grateful for _____

I am grateful for _____

I am grateful for _____

I am grateful for _____

I am grateful for _____

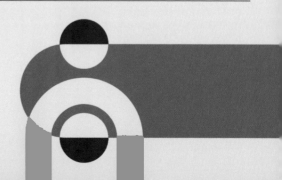

DAY 2

I am grateful for _____

I am grateful for _____

I am grateful for _____

I am grateful for _____

I am grateful for _____

DAY 3

I am grateful for _____

I am grateful for _____

I am grateful for _____

I am grateful for _____

I am grateful for _____

DAY 4

I am grateful for _____

I am grateful for _____

I am grateful for _____

I am grateful for _____

I am grateful for _____

MY SEVEN-DAY GRATITUDE PRACTICE

DAY 5

I am grateful for _____

I am grateful for _____

I am grateful for _____

I am grateful for _____

I am grateful for _____

DAY 6

I am grateful for _____

I am grateful for _____

I am grateful for _____

I am grateful for _____

I am grateful for _____

DAY 7

I am grateful for _____

I am grateful for _____

I am grateful for _____

I am grateful for _____

I am grateful for _____

FIVE GRATITUDE INTENTIONS

After your seven-day gratitude practice, fill in the blanks on this page with things you'd like to create in your daily life.

I am grateful for _____

I am grateful for _____

I am grateful for _____

I am grateful for _____

I am grateful for _____

It's really about taking one moment at a time and trying to master those moments.

—Serena Williams

CALMING TOOLS

The variety of changes that come with loss can be intimidating. Moreover, you may find yourself reacting to people, places, and things differently from before. As you traverse the bumpy terrain of loss, know that it is important to treat yourself with love, kindness, and compassion.

You may enjoy new things and no longer enjoy things that you did before. During this time, it is reinvigorating to discover what you can do for yourself to relax and rejuvenate. This section includes activities for you to engage with to help ease your stress.

RECOGNIZING AND APPRECIATING

Take time to recognize and appreciate what makes you smile, feel good, experience relief, and be thankful.

I recognize _____

I recognize _____

I recognize _____

I recognize _____

I recognize _____

I recognize _____

I recognize _____

I recognize _____

I recognize _____

I recognize _____

RECOGNIZING AND APPRECIATING

I appreciate _____

I appreciate _____

I appreciate _____

I appreciate _____

I appreciate _____

I appreciate _____

I appreciate _____

I appreciate _____

I appreciate _____

I appreciate _____

HELPING OTHERS

Helping others and engaging in something that is bigger than ourselves can provide purpose in our lives. It can give us joy during challenging times and help keep us going. Service also helps our minds and bodies as well as speeds recovery. Below, write how you are or would like to be of service.

I AM OF SERVICE TO MY FAMILY BY:

I AM OF SERVICE AT HOME BY:

I AM OF SERVICE AT WORK BY:

I AM OF SERVICE IN MY NEIGHBORHOOD BY:

I AM OF SERVICE IN MY COMMUNITY BY:

HELPING OTHERS

Being of service also connects us with others, making us a part of a team. On this page, write about any groups you are part of or would like to be a part of and how they contribute to others.

MEMBERS OF MY HOME TEAM ARE:

WE CONTRIBUTE BY:

MEMBERS OF MY WORK TEAM ARE:

WE CONTRIBUTE BY:

MEMBERS OF MY COMMUNITY TEAMS ARE:

WE CONTRIBUTE BY:

BEING CREATIVE

The act of being creative is another powerful tool that lifts us up. A creative act can be anything from cooking, writing, singing, dancing, coloring, painting, building, gardening, and more. It can also be an athletic activity. The act of creating begins with imagining something and then doing it.

Creativity is a state of being in which one opens oneself to imagination, joy, and fun. Releasing ourselves into creativity allows us to regenerate, relax, regroup, and even relieve pain. The end result is the bonus. So, allow a childlike freedom to anything you choose. Create with abandon.

Circle creative activities that you like to do. If there is something you enjoy that is not on the list, add it!

- Acting
- Painting
- Collaging
- Dancing
- Singing
- Sewing
- Printmaking
- Baking
- Cooking
- Drawing
- Storytelling
- Sketching
- Video/ Filmmaking
- Photography
- Reading
- Gardening
- Wood carving
- Cake decorating
- Scrapbooking
- Building
- Sculpting
- Playing an instrument
- Playing games
- Running
- Exercising
- Golfing
- Skateboarding
- Swimming
- Podcasting
- Coloring

BEING CREATIVE

Select three activities from the previous page that you would like to do several times a week or even every day. List those activities below and write about how you feel when you are doing them. Remember, being creative is about the doing, not about the end product.

1)

2)

3)

ENGAGING IN CONSCIOUS BREATHING

Breathing is such a natural occurrence that for the most part, it happens without us having to think about it. For one week, spend some time every day quietly observing your breath. It can be as short as five minutes or as long as an hour. It is up to you.

To begin, sit or lie in a comfortable position, and set your timer. Then gently close your eyes and pay attention to your breath. Is it even, steady, or does it fluctuate? When you're ready, add intention to your breathing. Start by taking deep, slow inhalations and exhalations through your nose. Notice the quality of your breath. Does it stay slow? What happens when your mind wanders? Does it change pace when you notice feelings of anxiousness, sadness, and anger? Capture your thoughts and experiences in the chart. After completing this activity, remember to use conscious breathing to calm and reinvigorate yourself throughout the day.

DAY	OBSERVATIONS	DAY	OBSERVATIONS
1		5	
2		6	
3		7	
4			

MOMENTS OF MEDITATING

When there is that oceanlike wave of sadness and upset, it is painful mentally, emotionally, and physically. Take note of where you are experiencing these emotions in your body. Engaging in conscious breathing and meditation at this moment can help reduce the stress and recenter oneself. Here is a short, brief meditation to do during moments when upset arises.

Sit or lie down in a comfortable space. Begin by taking three long, slow, smooth inhalations through your nose and three long, smooth exhalations through your nose. Pause and notice your feelings. Continue and complete three more deep breaths. Observe how your body is feeling. Then close your eyes and use your mind to go outside yourself. Picture a favorite location you've visited or would like to visit. Notice the colors, the sounds, and the smells. Experience the energy of this space. Notice once again how your body is feeling. When you feel yourself returning to a calmer state, slowly open your eyes and reengage with your life.

LISTENING TO MUSIC

Music is not only pleasant but can retrain your nerves to find calm and peace in difficult times. Here are some ideas of how you can tap into the creativity of music to help yourself feel good.

- Select music you enjoy and that relaxes you. Classical music, jazz, soft rock, country, opera, and hip hop can all be soothing.
- Have this music nearby and ready to play, especially in places where your negative emotions can be triggered, like in the car during heavy traffic situations.
- Give yourself permission to sing along or hum as loud as you'd like.
- Dance to the music until your heart's content.
- Allow the music to touch your heart and soul.

LISTENING TO MUSIC

Identify specific songs you like to listen to that elevate your mood. Then select specific times during the day to listen. Listen to these songs during your chosen time of day for a week.

DAY	MUSIC TITLE	TIME OF DAY	FEELINGS
Monday			
Tuesday			
Wednesday			
Thursday			
Friday			
Saturday			
Sunday			

THINGS THAT CALM & RELAX ME

Reflect on your experiences using the resilience-building activities and write about how you felt doing each one. Identify which tools you found most useful and record why on the lines below.

- ☐ Recognizing and Appreciating
- ☐ Being Creative
- ☐ Engaging in Conscious Breathing
- ☐ Moments of Meditating
- ☐ Listening to Music

_____

_____

_____

_____

_____

_____

_____

_____

_____

_____

_____

THINGS THAT CALM & RELAX ME

Make a plan to incorporate the activities in the chart into your daily or weekly routine.

RESILIENCE TOOL	DAYS OF THE WEEK	TIME ALLOCATED
Recognizing and Appreciating		
Being Creative		
Engaging in Conscious Breathing		
Moments of Meditating		
Listening to Music		

What you do for yourself, any gesture of kindness, any gesture of gentleness, any gesture of honesty and clear seeing toward yourself, will affect how you experience your world. In fact, it will transform how you experience the world. What you do for yourself, you're doing for others, and what you do for others, you're doing for yourself.

—Pema Chödrön

TAKING CARE OF MYSELF

Taking care of yourself begins with being kind to yourself. During this time, treat yourself as you would a dear family member or friend going through hardship. Show yourself that warmth and compassion you normally reserve for others.

Getting started in taking care of yourself can be a challenge—especially after so many changes. It's normal to feel unsure or find difficulty at first. These pages help with that by laying out where and how to begin to take care of yourself. If you are still finding it difficult, ask someone to help jumpstart your self-care.

REACHING OUT: CONNECTIONS AND RECONNECTIONS

There are so many ways to communicate these days: text, email, phone, social media, and the list goes on. Many forms of communication simply pass information rather than create connection. Couple that with the hurdles of loss, and reaching out can make one feel uncomfortably vulnerable. These steps will assist you in overcoming common barriers to connection.

STEP ONE: Make a list of people you'd like to contact.

STEP TWO: Reach out to two people every week.

STEP THREE: Invite at least one person to get together with and make plans to do so. Schedule a short, informal, low-pressure situation for you to have face-to-face interaction with them (for example, having coffee, breakfast, or lunch, or taking a walk or run).

STEP FOUR: Take it slow and easy. Do not feel like you need to be as engaged as usual. However, a little connection on a regular basis (even if you don't feel like it) can really help you to feel better.

STEP FIVE: Accept invitations that you are really interested in. It may take time, often several months or more, before you feel like getting out much. In the beginning, resist the urge to say yes to everything because you don't want to disappoint friends and family. Let them know that you appreciate them including you, but a little at a time works best for a while.

FAMILY MEMBERS	REACHED OUT	DATE TO CONNECT

FRIENDS	REACHED OUT	DATE TO CONNECT

COLLEAGUES & WORK ASSOCIATES	REACHED OUT	DATE TO CONNECT

PEOPLE YOU JUST MET	REACHED OUT	DATE TO CONNECT

REESTABLISH AND CREATE
DAILY ROUTINES & PRACTICES

On these pages, capture your new daily routines for each day of the week. Much has changed, so write down what you are currently doing as well as what you want to be doing and when. Include what you do in the morning upon waking, through the day, and in the evening. Don't forget to include your time to rest and relax.

TIME	SUNDAY	MONDAY	TUESDAY

REESTABLISH AND CREATE
DAILY ROUTINES & PRACTICES

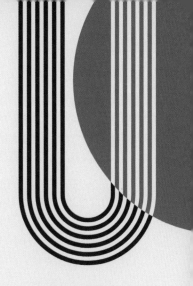

WEDNESDAY	THURSDAY	FRIDAY	SATURDAY

SLEEP TRACKER

The body and mind need sleep to recover. However, during particularly stressful times, sleep patterns often are disrupted. To be aware of this, keep track of how much real sleep you are getting and the quality of sleep for two weeks.

Record the number of hours slept, the degree of ease or difficulty of going to sleep and getting up in the morning, and the continuity of sleep. Also note the number of times you wake during the night and the ease or difficulty of going back to sleep.

DAY	TIME SLEPT	SLEEP QUALITY
Monday		
Tuesday		
Wednesday		
Thursday		
Friday		
Saturday		
Sunday		

DAY	TIME SLEPT	SLEEP QUALITY
Monday		
Tuesday		
Wednesday		
Thursday		
Friday		
Saturday		
Sunday		

MY EXERCISE TRACKER

Regular exercise is not only healthy for the body but also for the mind. The idea of regular exercise can be daunting, so use the exercise tracker on these pages to make it easier to get started and keep going. Make a commitment to yourself to exercise every day for 30 days and record what each day's exercise was. If you need to, put a reminder on your phone to make sure you remember to do your exercise. On the really challenging days, your exercise might be a walk to the corner and back, which is okay. It is helpful to do something every day, even if it is just a little.

DAY 1 _____

DAY 2 _____

DAY 3 _____

DAY 4 _____

DAY 5 _____

DAY 6 _____

DAY 7 _____

DAY 8 _____

DAY 9 _____

DAY 10 _____

DAY 11 _____

DAY 12 _____

DAY 13 _____

DAY 14 _____

DAY 15 _____

DAY 16 _____

DAY 17 _____

DAY 18 _____

DAY 19 _____

DAY 20 _____

DAY 22 _____

DAY 23 _____

DAY 24 _____

DAY 25 _____

DAY 26 _____

DAY 27 _____

DAY 28 _____

DAY 29 _____

DAY 30 _____

People are like stained-glass windows. They sparkle and shine when the sun is out, but when the darkness sets in, their true beauty is revealed only if there is light from within.

—Elisabeth Kübler-Ross

MY RECOVERY TIME

After a significant loss, our bodies and minds need time to recover. The challenge is how to do that when our lives are filled with activities, commitments, and expectations. Shortening or ignoring recovery can actually extend how long it takes to adapt, adjust, and transition. By understanding and accepting how important it is to recover, plus a little bit of planning, we can build recovery time into our daily lives.

WHEN I NEED A QUICK SOLUTION (BUILD INTO EVERY DAY)

Here are some simple, easy, and effective approaches to use during transitions when recovery is essential. Choose two or three tools so that you have multiple options to turn to when the stress builds.

- Find a few minutes of uninterrupted peace and quiet to be alone every day.

- Close your eyes and see in your mind's eye a favorite location. Imagine being there.

- Take several five- to ten-minute breaks during the day.

- Turn your cell phone and all other devices off for at least 10 minutes every day.

- Take a walk around the block.

- Plan some downtime between commitments.

- Throughout the day, take three long, deep, smooth breaths in and out through your nose.

WHEN I NEED A QUICK SOLUTION (BUILD INTO EVERY DAY)

Create your personal list of five to ten daily quick recovery fixes to incorporate into your daily life. Do your best to make them a part of everyday routine.

WHEN I NEED A LITTLE MORE (BUILD INTO THE WEEK)

To reinforce your recovery time, here are some longer, yet still manageable activities to build into the week. Choose two or three activities.

- Exercise. For example, take a short, fun, vigorous walk, lift weights, or do yoga.

- Listen to your favorite music.

- Spend 30 minutes doing something you enjoy, just because you enjoy it.

- Spend 30 minutes in nature—walking, hiking, or just sitting and being.

- Prepare and enjoy your favorite food.

- Meditate—it could be a five-minute meditation or a longer meditation. It is up to you.

- Turn a chore into a game.

- Watch a favorite movie.

- Read a book.

WHEN I NEED A LITTLE MORE (BUILD INTO THE WEEK)

Create your personal list of five recovery actions to build into your week. Include the day or time of when you plan to do the actions to help structure and incorporate the actions into your week.

-

-

-

-

-

WHEN I NEED EVEN MORE (BUILD INTO THE MONTH)

Strengthen your recovery by setting aside some extended time for yourself each month. Choose two or three activities from the suggestions below to care for yourself.

- Binge watch favorite shows or movies.
- Spend a weekend away from home.
- Go hiking, fishing, camping, or all three.
- Have dinner at your favorite restaurant.
- Go to a movie or theater.
- Do one of your favorite activities and don't let anything interfere with that time.

WHEN I NEED EVEN MORE
(BUILD INTO THE MONTH)

Create your personal list of at least five recovery actions to build into the month. Include the day or time of when you plan to do the actions to help incorporate the activities into your life.

1) _____

DAY & TIME _____

2) _____

DAY & TIME _____

3) _____

DAY & TIME _____

4) _____

DAY & TIME _____

5) _____

DAY & TIME _____

This is where it all begins.
Everything starts here, today.

—David Nicholls

GETTING GOING AGAIN

Now this can feel like a tough challenge. How can I get into action when my heart is so sad, my fear so overwhelming, and all action so heavy? It is not easy, but with practice, it can become more so. Take it one step at a time, one action at a time, and one day at a time. Most importantly, be gentle and compassionate with yourself. Simultaneously be the coach who makes you do it and the trusted friend who tells you how well you are doing.

THE IMPORTANCE OF FUN

During tough times, especially when we are processing our grief and adjusting to our loss, having fun is something that eludes us. Why should I have fun after what has happened? Research reveals that smiling, laughter, and fun are all good for you. Even when it doesn't feel easy or natural to do, it is essential to your well-being.

Without thinking too much about it, fill in the blanks to the prompts below with the first thing that comes to mind.

When I was a child, for fun I would...

_____

When I was a child, for fun I would...

_____

When I was a child, for fun I would...

_____

As I was growing up, my favorite things to do were...

_____

As I was growing up, my favorite things to do were...

_____

As I was growing up, my favorite things to do were...

_____

THINGS I LIKE TO DO, JUST BECAUSE

Think for a moment about the things you do, just because you like to them. It can be anything and everything, from making a delicious cup of coffee to playing video games, and everything in between. If your response right now is nothing, then reach into your memories and retrieve the activities from there.

About my daily activities, I like to...

_____

About my daily activities, I like to...

_____

About my daily activities, I like to...

_____

About my favorite activities, I really enjoy...

_____

About my favorite activities, I really enjoy...

_____

About my favorite activities, I really enjoy...

_____

THINGS THAT MAKE ME SMILE

Think about the things you do that make you smile, laugh, and feel good. Capture them all here.

I FIND MYSELF SMILING AT:

I FIND MYSELF SMILING WHEN:

PEOPLE, PETS & THINGS THAT MAKE ME LAUGH

Now think about the people, pets, and things that you enjoy and make you laugh. List them below. It could be family, friends, colleagues, celebrities, performers, pets, and other animals. Also consider books, movies, shows, podcasts, games, and athletic activities.

-
-
-
-
-
-
-
-
-
-

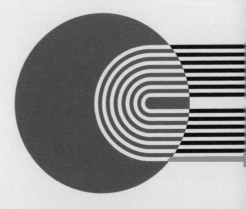

PEOPLE I ENJOY BEING WITH

Recall experiences and events that you really enjoyed and remember who you were there with. Fill in the blanks on these pages with the names of people you like being around. For example, it can be the barista at your regular café or your closest friend. These are people to think about reaching out to and interacting with to support you during this time.

PEOPLE I CONSIDER FAMILY

_____

_____

_____

_____

MY FRIENDS

_____

_____

_____

_____

PEOPLE I INTERACT WITH DAILY

_____

_____

_____

_____

CO-WORKERS

_____

_____

_____

_____

NEIGHBORS

_____

_____

_____

_____

MEMBERS OF MY COMMUNITIES

_____

_____

_____

_____

UNCOVERING & REDISCOVERING INTERESTS

What do you love to do? Think about the things that you do from a place of joy. Incorporating those activities into your daily life can make a difference between wanting to get out of bed in the morning or not. How much time you allocate to spend on these endeavors will vary, based on other commitments and responsibilities. The magic of pursuing your passions is not dependent on how much time you put in—as little as 10 minutes every day will make a difference.

List activities and/or hobbies you love doing.

-
-
-
-
-

Now list them again beginning with the one you enjoy the most.

-
-
-
-
-

UNCOVERING & REDISCOVERING INTERESTS

For the next 30 days, track how much time you spend doing one or more of these activities. Try spending at least 10 minutes a day on one activity. For a musician, that might be playing your instrument; for a mechanic, it might be working on a car; for a cook, it might be finding new recipes to try. It is uplifting to do even a little every day.

DAY	MINUTES	DAY	MINUTES
1		16	
2		17	
3		18	
4		19	
5		20	
6		21	
7		22	
8		23	
9		24	
10		25	
11		26	
12		27	
13		28	
14		29	
15		30	

UNCOVERING NEW INTERESTS

Sometimes identifying what we love to do is challenging because we've changed and things we used to love just don't feel the same anymore. The next few pages include a step-by-step exercise that helps uncover and recognize new interest(s) that connect us to happiness. Dream big!

UNCOVERING NEW INTERESTS

STEP 1: FIND IT

Close your eyes and picture a magic wand in your hand. When you wave it, you can do anything you want to do. Wave it now. What is the first thing you see? Remember, this is about doing something you really want to do for the pure joy of doing it. You are not doing this for accomplishment—though that tends to follow. Ignore any "I can't" thoughts or other negative self-talk.

Now think about what you created with your magic wand. How does it make you feel? Are you moved by it? If not, repeat the exercise and look again to find that idea or interest that comes to mind, the thing that you would usually rule out before even considering it. Keep repeating the exercise until you uncover it.

I WOULD LOVE TO:

_____

_____

_____

_____

_____

Congratulations! You have completed the first step. It takes courage to go after your dreams.

UNCOVERING NEW INTERESTS

STEP 2: DREAMS INTO ACTION

We've all heard stories about people who successfully pursue their passions in spite of a lack of resources: the artist who makes art out of found items from the side of the road, the athlete who trains outside, the writer who does not have access to a device and uses paper and pencil. Doors open when you put yourself on the path.

Now identify a small action you can take on your passion's path. Any step, no matter how small, will make a huge difference. Some suggestions for a step are to tell a friend or loved one you are going to start doing this new activity, research the interest online, take a class, join an organization, and find information that inspires you.

MY ACTION IS _____
_____
_____

STEP 3: GO DO IT

Now for the fun part—do the action! Once you do, you'll find that dreams can become reality if we take the step.

I TOOK MY ACTION ON _____
_____
_____

UNCOVERING NEW INTERESTS

STEP 4: WEEKLY CHECK-IN

Make a plan for each week and record at least one action you've taken toward pursuing your passion, no matter how small. At first it may be difficult, but start small. Eventually the process will take over, and before you know it you'll have incorporated your passion into your life.

WEEK	ACTION
1	
2	
3	
4	
5	
6	
7	
8	
9	
10	

Imagination is more important than knowledge.

—Albert Einstein

MY VISION & DREAMS FOR MY FUTURE

In this section, you will dream your most heartfelt dreams. Imagine, create, and capture those thoughts. There are only a few rules:

1) Create only things you really want.

2) Design a life that gets you out of bed in the morning, even on the tough days.

3) Do not self-edit, even when it comes to resources or rationale.

4) Be real and authentic, and speak from your heart.

5) Capture all of it on these next pages.

After you finish this section, let it sit overnight before returning to these pages. Make any changes you'd like and then move on to the rest of the journal where you will focus on bringing your dreams to life—your life. Feel good and have fun!

MY VISION & DREAMS FOR MY FUTURE

WHAT I WANT MY FAMILY TO LOOK LIKE:

WHO I WANT IT TO INCLUDE:

MY VISION & DREAMS FOR MY FUTURE

MY IMPORTANT RELATIONSHIPS ARE WITH:

THE RELATIONSHIPS ARE LIKE THIS:

MY VISION & DREAMS FOR MY FUTURE

THE TYPE OF WORK/CAREER I WANT TO BE DOING IS:

IDEAS I HAVE TO HELP ME PURSUE THAT WORK ARE:

MY VISION & DREAMS FOR MY FUTURE

I'D LIKE TO BE LIVING IN:

CITY _____

STATE _____

MY HOME WILL BE:

MY NEIGHBORHOOD WILL BE:

MY VISION & DREAMS FOR MY FUTURE

MY NEIGHBORS ARE:

I AM INVOLVED IN THESE COMMUNITIES:

MY VISION & DREAMS FOR MY FUTURE

IN ONE YEAR, MY LIFE WILL LOOK LIKE:

IN FIVE YEARS, MY LIFE WILL LOOK LIKE:

IN TEN YEARS, MY LIFE WILL LOOK LIKE:

Follow your bliss and the universe will open doors where there were only walls.

—Joseph Campbell

CREATING & EXECUTING MY PLANS

Sometimes it can feel overwhelming to figure out what we want to do and then get started. This section will gently guide you through a process to assist you in identifying and executing the next steps toward your goals.

GOALS AND RESOURCES

When experiencing the weight of loss and the sadness of grief, one is susceptible to inertia. These next few pages are designed to make it easier to get going in this new chapter of your life.

Set goals for your life for the next 12 months.

1) _____

2) _____

3) _____

4) _____

5) _____

Identify resources (people, organizations, services) that can help you move toward those goals.

1) _____

2) _____

3) _____

4) _____

5) _____

6) _____

7) _____

8) _____

9) _____

10) _____

REACHING OUT

Now that you've made a list of resources, contact those resources. Be clear about what you are looking for before you reach out. When someone is of assistance to you, be sure to send an email, note, or card expressing your appreciation. Fill out the chart below with the names of people you have reached out to, and write down any and all next steps in following up.

CALL OR EMAIL THE FOLLOWING PEOPLE	YOUR FOLLOW-UPS

POSITIVE RESPONSES & RESULTS

Fill in this page with positive responses you hear from sharing your goals and, as a result, how you are moving forward.

RESPONSE	RESULTS

NEXT STEPS & TIMING

Record and track what you need to do next and when.

NEXT STEPS	TIMING

Only in the reality of the present can we love, can we awaken, can we find peace and understanding and connection with ourselves and the world.

—Jack Kornfield

MY REFLECTIONS

In these final pages, capture your learnings, experiences, thoughts, and feelings. Make sure to write down your insights and identify which practices work best for you. Record how you have or are going to incorporate these activities into your life.

MY PRIVATE REFLECTIONS

I AM FEELING:

MY PRIVATE REFLECTIONS

I AM NOTICING:

_____

_____

_____

_____

_____

_____

_____

_____

_____

_____

_____

_____

_____

_____

_____

_____

_____

_____

_____

LOVE LINES TO MYSELF & OTHERS

There is never too much giving and receiving love. On these pages are expressions of kindness and appreciation for you to remember to share with yourself and people you care about.

- I appreciate you.
- I really appreciate all you do for me.
- I appreciate your generosity.
- I appreciate your support.
- I appreciate your kindness.
- I appreciate your patience.
- I appreciate your sense of humor.
- I appreciate your love.
- I love you.
- I admire you.
- I miss you.
- You bring out the best in me.
- You give the best hugs.
- You are my role model.

LOVE LINES TO MYSELF & OTHERS

- You understand me.
- You inspire me.
- You are the best.
- You are the light in my life.
- You are amazing.
- You are my rock.
- You are everything to me.
- Thank you for being there for me.
- Thank you for believing in me.
- Thank you for doing everything you do.
- Thank you for caring enough about me to say no.
- Thank you for accepting me.
- Thank you for trusting me.
- Thank you for being you.
- Thank you for loving me, just the way I am.
- Thank you for making me laugh.

LETTER TO MYSELF

These pages are for you to write a letter to yourself to read one year from today. Write from your heart. Write about the special moments that inspired you, the kindnesses you experienced, and your accomplishments from the year. Create the year that you desire as you move forward. Share what you appreciate from your daily life and acknowledge people who you love.

Dear Me,

_____

_____

_____

_____

_____

_____

_____

_____

_____

_____

_____

_____

_____

MY PRACTICES

Review your journal, select the tools you most enjoyed, and list them here. Write a little about how they made you feel. Then circle the practices that you are going to commit to adding to your daily life.

-

-

One More Day

One more day.
The thought reaches me, but I do not
fully understand the significance of it.

One more day.
The realization begins to creep up on me
through the cracks and porches of my mind.

One more day.
I feel a surge of happiness, a surge of hope,
a surge of... relief.

One more day.
Capping the hard work and the struggle that
we all have to endure in our own way.

One more day.
When we realize what it was all for.

And one more day.

—C. Wilburn

RECOMMENDED READING

DeSpelder, Lynne Ann and Albert Lee Strickland. *The Last Dance: Encountering Death and Dying*. New York: McGraw-Hill Education, 2011.

Hillman, James. *Re-Visioning psychology*. New York: Harper Perennial, 1992.

Hillman, James. *The Soul's Code: In Search of Character and Calling*. New York: Random House, 1996.

Kessler, David. *Finding Meaning: The Sixth Stage of Grief*. New York: Simon & Schuster, 2019.

Kübler-Ross, Elizabeth and David Kessler. *On Grief & Grieving: Finding the Meaning of Grief Through the Five Stages of Loss*. New York: Simon & Schuster, 2005.

Mundy, Michaelene and R.W. Alley. *Sad Isn't Bad: A Good-grief Guidebook for Kids Dealing with Loss*. St. Meinrad, Indiana: CareNotes, 1998.

Remen, Rachel Naomi. *Kitchen Table Wisdom: Stories That Heal*. New York: Riverhead Books, 1996.

VanDuivendyk, Tim P. *The Unwanted Gift of Grief: A Ministry Approach*. New York: Psychology Press, 2006.

ACKNOWLEDGMENTS

My deepest gratitude to everyone recognized here, who without their support I would never have undertaken the Resiliency Guide series. First, I am grateful for my family. Christian your resilience, kindness, and daily practices inspire me. I am grateful for your "one writer to another" encouragement and your completely honest editorial comments. Having your support during this unforeseen and highly challenging year made it possible for me to fulfill my dream of sharing this life-altering information with as many people as possible. I am so grateful for you!

I am grateful for all my teachers during this 24-year healing journey. I am truly at a loss for words to describe the depth of my appreciation for you being there to instruct, assist, and remind me to practice. I am grateful for my yoga teacher never giving up on my healing goals when everyone else did, and for the dignity and respect with which you treat me. I am grateful for Pam Lanza & Glenn Hirsch who helped me become an artist when I could barely move my hands and arms. I miss you both, may you rest in peace. I am grateful for Dr. Maud Nerman and Adrienne Larkin for role modeling that healing is a lifelong journey and to never give up.

A deep heartfelt thank you to my friends and colleagues who stood with me during these many challenging years, enthusiastically encouraging my writing, art, and studies. I am grateful for my dear friend Faith Winthrop. I will celebrate with you in my heart. I am grateful for my dear friends Laurie McFarlane, Aiko Morioka, and Cathy River for your unshakable support. I am grateful for Gordon Sumner, Karen Leveque, Matt Schwartz, and John Kirkpatrick for supporting me in so many ways. I am grateful for the people around the world who trust me daily with their joys, fears, accomplishments, hurts, and their hearts. I am privileged to be of service to you!

I am grateful for those of you whose stellar work helped bring the Resiliency Guides into existence. I am grateful for my research assistant, Luke Schwartz. I am grateful for the inspiring team at West Margin Press. I am grateful for Jen Newens for understanding the work and providing the platform for this information to reach so many others. I am grateful for Olivia Ngai's detailed, precise, and inspired editing. I am grateful for Rachel Metzger's innovative designs capturing and reflecting the heart of these books. I am grateful for Angie Zbornik's and Alice Wertheimer's strategic marketing ideas, innovative execution, support, and patience as I focused on the content. I deeply appreciate all your work!

ABOUT THE AUTHOR

Janine Wilburn is an award-winning artist, innovator, and writer. She has a master's degree in East West Psychology and is pursuing her PhD. For decades, Janine worked as a marketing professional, receiving recognition for her work with a Cannes Film Festival Bronze Lion, a Clio, and other awards, until a car accident changed her life. Suffering spinal damage, she needed to heal. Through her studies in neuroscience, neuroplasticity, yoga, and meditation, Janine persevered and developed resilience-building practices. The Resiliency Guides are the result of her research, experience, hope, and commitment to help others. Janine lives in San Francisco, California.

I dedicate this book to all those courageously journeying their way through loss.

This book is not intended to diagnose or replace any medical advice or information. The publisher and author do not make any warranties about the completeness, reliability, or accuracy of the information in these pages. The publisher and author are not responsible and are not liable for any damages or negative consequences from any treatment, action, or application to any person reading or following the information in this book.

Text © 2022 by Janine Wilburn

Art Credits: Koru by Kate Bourke from the Noun Project; Kanate / Shutterstock.com; arvec / Shutterstock.com

ISBN: 9781513209586

Printed in China
1 2 3 4 5

Published by West Margin Press

**WEST
MARGIN
PRESS**
WestMarginPress.com

Proudly distributed by Ingram Publisher Services

WEST MARGIN PRESS
Publishing Director: Jennifer Newens
Marketing Manager: Alice Wertheimer
Project Specialist: Micaela Clark
Editor: Olivia Ngai
Design & Production: Rachel Lopez Metzger